TRAVELLING
ON LAND

DEBORAH CHANCELLOR

In association with
FRANKLIN WATTS

How to use this book

Cross references
Above the heading on the page, you will find a list of subjects in the book which are connected to the topic. Look at these pages to find out more about the subjects.

See for yourself
See for yourself bubbles give you the chance to test out some of the ideas in this book. They explain what you will need and what you have to do to see if an idea really works.

Quiz corner
In the quiz corner, you will find a list of questions. The answers to the quiz questions are somewhere on the two pages. Can you answer all the questions about each topic?

Glossary
Difficult words are explained in the glossary near the back of the book. These words are in **bold** on the page. Look them up in the glossary to find out what they mean.

Index
The index is at the back of the book. It is a list of words about everything mentioned in the book, with page numbers next to the words. The list is in the same order as the alphabet. If you want to find out about a subject, look up the word in the index, then turn to the page number given.

Contents

Animal power

Thousands of years ago, the only way to travel was by walking. Then people learned to ride animals from one place to another. Travelling became much easier when an ancient people, called the Sumerians, invented the wheel. Animals could now pull carts carrying people and loads. Today, animals still help people to travel and do their work.

Inventing the wheel

The first wheels were made of solid wood. They were strong, but heavy and turned slowly. Over time, half-solid wheels were made. These were lighter and turned more easily. Wheels with **spokes** are the lightest wheels of all, and as strong as solid ones.

Taming animals

Before most animals can carry loads or people, they must be tamed and trained. An animal that pulls a cart is taught to wear a harness that fixes it to the cart.

▲ These horses are pulling a stagecoach, full of passengers and their baggage.

▼ Llamas have cloven, or split, hooves, which help them to grip as they travel along mountain paths.

Working animals

In many parts of the world, people use animals to do work that they find difficult. Some animals, such as elephants, can move loads that are too heavy for people to carry. Other animals, such as llamas and camels, are useful because they can travel to places that cars and trucks cannot reach.

Quiz Corner

- How did people travel before the wheel was invented?

- What are animals taught to wear before they can pull a cart?

- Which large animal is good at moving heavy loads?

▲ These elephants in Thailand have been trained to move heavy logs with their trunks.

5

look at: Motorbikes, page 8

Bicycles

A bicycle is a simple machine that has two wheels. You make it move by turning the pedals with your feet. A bicycle is cheap to run and does not **pollute** the air. This is because it has no **engine**. All around the world, adults and children ride bicycles, especially in places where cars cannot go.

*Changing to a low **gear** makes it easier for the rider to pedal uphill.*

The handlebars let the rider steer and balance the bike.

The brakes rub against the wheel to slow down the bike.

▲ This cyclist is stunt-riding. He is wearing padded clothing, a helmet and safety goggles to protect himself if he falls off.

An American called Steve Roberts has invented the world's strangest bicycle. It has four computers and a fridge on board, which are all powered by the Sun's rays.

*The chain carries **power** to the back wheel and makes the wheel turn.*

*To help the tyres grip the road, they have a rough pattern on them, called the **tread**.*

The pedals are linked to the back wheel by the chain.

Bikes for hire

In some countries, people use cycle rickshaws to travel about town. These are similar to bicycles but usually have three wheels. People pay the rickshaw driver to take them to where they want to go.

▲ Often, it is quicker and cheaper to travel by cycle rickshaw than by car.

Quiz Corner

- Do bicycles pollute the air?
- What does a bicycle chain do?
- Which part of a bicycle lets you steer and helps you to balance?
- What is the pattern on a tyre called?

look at: Bicycles, page 6

Motorbikes

A motorbike is similar to a bicycle, but it has a petrol **engine** to make it move. It is also stronger than a bicycle and can travel faster. In 1885, the first motorbike was built in Germany by Gottlieb Daimler. It could travel at 12km per hour. Today, motorbikes can reach much higher speeds. The world record is 513km per hour.

CHATTERBOX

How many people do you think can balance on one motorbike? In 1987, in New South Wales, Australia, 47 people managed to ride on a single bike.

A biker must wear a helmet to protect his head in case of an accident. ....

A shield made of tough, clear plastic protects the biker from the wind. ....

A biker wears strong leather clothing to protect his body and keep him warm. ....

Gripping the ground

As a motorbike moves along, rough **tread** on the tyre causes **friction** between the tyre and the ground. Friction helps the tyre to grip the ground.

▼ The tyres on a trail bike have an especially deep tread to help them grip rough, wet and muddy ground.

Trail bikes

Not all motorbikes are built to be ridden on roads. A trail bike can travel across country, even in places where there are no dirt tracks. It can also climb hills and cross streams.

Tread on the tyres gives more grip on wet roads.

Quiz Corner

● Who built the first motorbike?

● Why do motorbike tyres have tread?

● Which kinds of motorbike can climb hills and cross streams?

look at: Roads, page 20, In the future, page 28

Cars

One of the easiest and quickest ways to travel is by car. Like motorbikes, most cars have petrol **engines**. Inside the engine, petrol burns to make **energy** which moves the car forwards. The first car with a petrol engine was built in 1885 by a German called Karl Benz. It had three wheels and travelled very slowly.

Streamlined cars
Engineers try to design cars with a **streamlined**, or smooth and rounded, shape. Streamlined cars let air flow over them easily, helping them to travel quickly. Cars that are not streamlined travel more slowly and use up more **fuel**.

In most cars, the engine is at the front of the car, under the bonnet.

At night, drivers use big headlights to see the road ahead. Indicator lights at the side of the car show when it is about to turn left or right.

Drivers use the steering wheel to turn the car.

Seat belts help to protect drivers and passengers if they are in an accident.

NY 3710

Designed for speed

A racing car has a very streamlined shape because it needs to travel at high speeds. The driver sits strapped into a snug seat.

◀ During a race, mechanics work quickly to change the car's tyres and fill it up with fuel.

Busy roads

Today, there are more cars on the road than ever before. In cities around the world, such as Los Angeles, in the USA, there are sometimes so many cars on the road, nobody can move. This is called gridlock.

At night, back lights make sure the car can be seen from behind.

Quiz Corner

- Who built the first car with a petrol engine?
- Why must racing cars have a streamlined shape?
- What is it called when there are so many cars on the road that nobody can move?

look at: Cars, page 10, Trains, page 22, In the future, page 28

Buses and trams

If more people travelled by bus than by car, there would be less traffic on the roads. Buses carry lots of people at one time along the same **route**. They are good for short journeys around town and for travelling long distances. One bus uses less **fuel** than if all the people on board travelled in their own cars.

Public transport

Most cities have a group of buses that people pay to use. This is one type of public transport. Each bus follows a different route, usually marked by a different number. People wait for the bus along the route at a bus stop. When people get on the bus, they buy a ticket to pay for their journey.

▼ This bus is on a route through London, in the UK. It has two **decks** and can carry about 90 people.

Long-distance travel

Some large buses, called coaches, travel long distances, from one city to another. They are designed to make journeys as pleasant as possible. They have soft seats, toilets and sometimes even show videos on board.

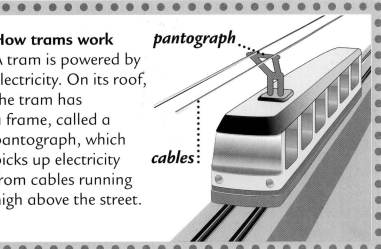

Trams

In some cities, such as San Francisco, in the USA, there are trams as well as buses. Trams run along steel rails which are sunk into the road. They are a good type of public transport because they cause little **pollution**.

How trams work

A tram is powered by electricity. On its roof, the tram has a frame, called a pantograph, which picks up electricity from cables running high above the street.

pantograph

cables

◀ Around the world, many buses are decorated and brightly coloured. They can be very crowded.

CHATTERBOX

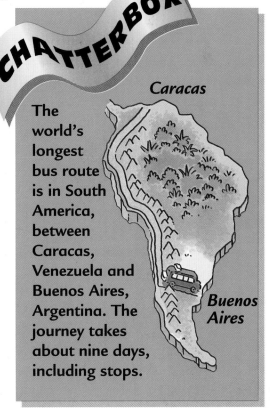

The world's longest bus route is in South America, between Caracas, Venezuela and Buenos Aires, Argentina. The journey takes about nine days, including stops.

Caracas

Buenos Aires

look at: Working trucks, page 16

Freight trucks

A **freight** truck is a large **vehicle** that carries heavy loads from one place to another by road. It is often the cheapest way to transport heavy loads. Different types of freight trucks carry different kinds of loads. Refrigerator trucks carry frozen foods. Inside, they have special equipment to keep the food ice-cold.

A powerful engine

A freight truck needs a powerful **engine** to carry its heavy load. A special hood behind the cab, called an air deflector, makes the truck more **streamlined**. This means that it uses less **fuel**. Most trucks run on a special fuel, called **diesel**.

▼ Before the driver begins a journey, mechanics make sure that the engine and wheels are working properly.

Articulated trucks

An articulated truck has two parts to make it easier to drive around corners. At the front, there is a cab and at the back, there is a long trailer. The two parts are joined by a hinge, which lets the driver's cab turn before the trailer.

air deflector

trailer

cab

▲ In Australia, massive trucks called road trains carry goods across the country. A road train can pull three trailers at a time.

Quiz Corner

- What is an articulated truck?
- In which part of a freight truck does the driver sit?
- Why do freight trucks need powerful engines?
- Which types of truck carry liquids?

▼ A car transporter is a long freight truck with two or more **decks**. It can carry many cars at one time.

Driving in style

Every year, a freight truck driver can drive thousands of kilometres, so the cab where he sits must be as comfortable as possible. Behind the driver's seat, there is often a special bed with a curtain around it, so the driver can take a rest when he needs to.

Liquid loads

A tanker is a freight truck that is specially built to carry liquids, such as milk or oil. The trailer on a tanker must be tightly sealed, so that it does not spill its load. The inside of the trailer is divided into separate sections to stop the liquid from splashing around.

look at: Freight trucks, page 14

Working trucks

There are many types of working truck and they all do different jobs. Refuse trucks carry rubbish away from people's houses, while diggers clear soil from the ground. In many places around the world, people, including builders and farmers, use working trucks to make their jobs easier.

A crane has an arm and hook for lifting heavy loads.

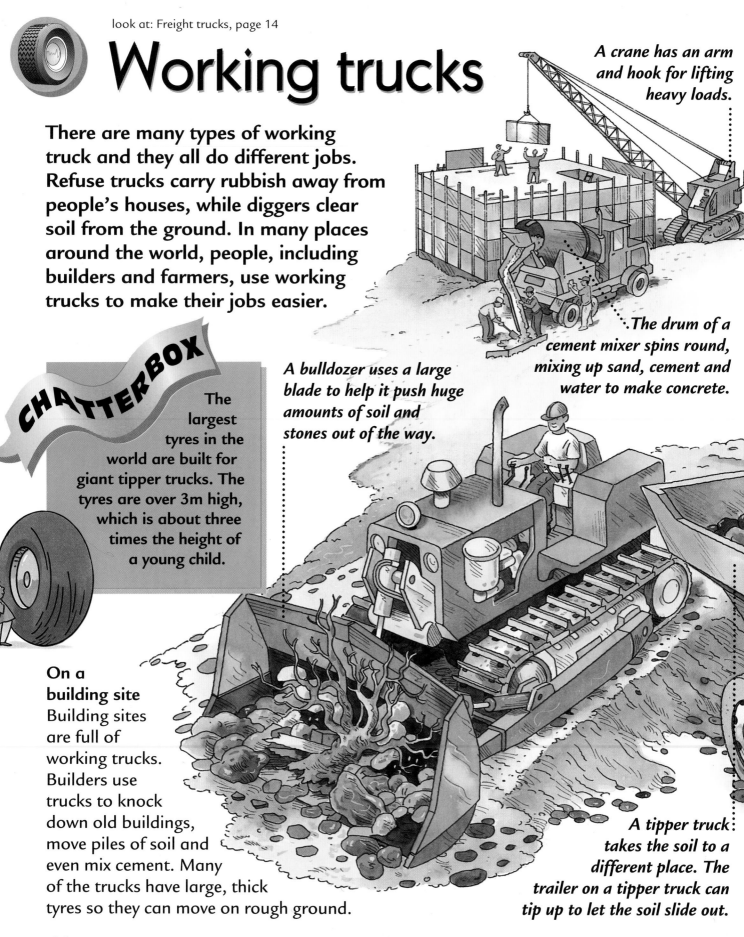

..The drum of a cement mixer spins round, mixing up sand, cement and water to make concrete.

A bulldozer uses a large blade to help it push huge amounts of soil and stones out of the way.

CHATTERBOX

The largest tyres in the world are built for giant tipper trucks. The tyres are over 3m high, which is about three times the height of a young child.

On a building site
Building sites are full of working trucks. Builders use trucks to knock down old buildings, move piles of soil and even mix cement. Many of the trucks have large, thick tyres so they can move on rough ground.

A tipper truck takes the soil to a different place. The trailer on a tipper truck can tip up to let the soil slide out.

On the farm

In the past, people or animals did all the heavy work on farms. Today, trucks, such as tractors and combine harvesters, are used instead. These machines work much faster than people or animals.

◀ A combine harvester does the work of many people. It cuts long lines of wheat and then separates the stalks from the grains.

A digger has a long arm that can bend to scoop up soil. It loads the soil on to a tipper truck.

Quiz Corner

● What are refuse trucks used for?

● How does a digger scoop up soil from the ground?

● Why do many farmers use trucks to help them with their work?

● What does a combine harvester do?

look at: Cars, page 10, Working trucks, page 16

In an emergency

When there is an emergency, such as an accident or a fire, special cars and trucks arrive to help. They must travel to the scene of the emergency as quickly as they can. These **vehicles** are all specially designed to do different jobs.

Fire engines

A fire engine is used to put out fires and rescue people trapped in buildings. It is packed with equipment, such as hoses, ladders, buckets and sand. Some fire engines carry huge amounts of water.

▶ Sometimes, firefighters use long ladders to rescue pets that are stuck in high trees.

A long ladder on the fire engine........... can reach to the tops of tall trees or buildings.

Firefighters must ... wear special clothes and hard hats to protect themselves from injury.

▲ A police car uses loud **sirens** and flashing lights to warn other drivers to keep out of its way when it is speeding along.

Emergency trucks are brightly coloured so people can see them easily. Try this test to see which colour is the brighter. Ask one friend to put on a pink T-shirt and another to put on a green one. Which T-shirt can you see more clearly from a distance?

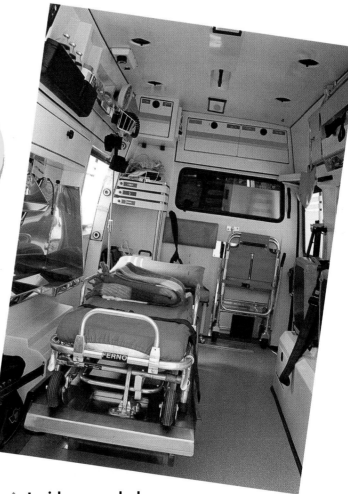

▲ Inside an ambulance, everything is designed so that the crew can reach it quickly.

Inside an ambulance

An ambulance is similar to a small hospital on wheels. Inside, it has life-saving equipment and medicines. It also has specially trained people on board. They carry sick people to the ambulance on a stretcher and look after them on their way to the hospital.

Automatic controls at the side of the fire engine can be used to raise and lower the ladder.

Quiz Corner

● Why do police cars have sirens and flashing lights?

● Why are emergency trucks always brightly coloured?

● What can you find inside an ambulance?

look at: Cars, page 10, In the future, page 28

Roads

A road is a strip of land that **vehicles** travel along. Thousands of years ago, long before cars were invented, the Romans were one of the first peoples to build roads. Carts travelled along these early roads, taking goods and people from one place to another. Today, roads cover most countries.

Road systems

Every town has roads which are connected to one another in a road system. People plan the road system carefully to make sure the traffic flows smoothly.

▼ Large cities are linked by motorways. These are big roads with a number of lanes. Cars can travel at high speeds on motorways.

Building a road

Modern roads are built in stages. First, the **route** is chosen. Then soil and rocks are moved away to make the ground flat. Next, the ground is packed down to make it firm, then covered with layers of gravel, concrete and steel wire mesh. Finally another layer of concrete or asphalt is put on top.

.... concrete
.... wire mesh
.... concrete
.... gravel
.... ground

To get on to a motorway, cars must travel along a slip road.

A flyover is a road that is built over the top of another road to let cars pass quickly.

Instead of driving over or around mountains, cars can travel through tunnels to make journeys quicker.

Steep roads on mountainsides have sharp, or hairpin, bends to help cars climb up hills.

Bridges let cars cross rivers and deep valleys.

Cars that do not want to visit the city centre can use a bypass to travel around the edge of the city.

Quiz Corner

● What is a flyover?

● How do you get on to a motorway?

● What are the stages in building a road?

● Who were one of the first peoples to build roads?

look at: Underground trains, page 24

Trains

A train is a long line of carriages, or cars, that carries people or goods. An **engine** pulls or pushes the train along a track. The first trains were powered by steam, but today they are usually powered by **diesel** or electricity. In 1825, the first steam railway opened in the UK. In those days, trains were slow and bumpy. Today, trains are usually much faster.

Keeping on track
A train has special wheels that help it to stay on the track. A lip, called a flange, sticks out from the inside edge of the wheel, and stops the train from sliding off the track.

flange

track . . . .

Modern trains
People are always trying to make better trains. A monorail train runs above the ground on a single raised rail. It is faster and cheaper to run than other trains. It is also much quieter because it has rubber wheels.

▼ Most monorail trains, such as this one in Sydney, Australia, are powered by electricity.

Quiz Corner

- Were the first trains powered by electricity or by steam?
- Why is the 'Rocket' famous?
- Which kind of train carries goods?
- Which kind of train travels on a single rail?

CHATTERBOX

Stephenson's 'Rocket' was the first steam engine to travel faster than a rider on horseback. In 1829, it won the world's first steam engine race.

Different kinds of trains

A **freight** train carries goods and a passenger train carries people. A freight train can have up to 200 cars, called wagons, and is longer than a passenger train.

▼ Freight trains transport goods on land quickly. Only aeroplanes can travel faster.

look at: Buses and trams, page 12, Trains, page 22

Underground trains

Many cities have underground railways. When the roads are busy, it is usually quicker and easier to travel below ground. Underground trains carry many passengers at one time. They do not cause **pollution** or traffic jams.

CHATTERBOX

When the underground in London, in the UK, first opened, it used steam-powered trains. The smoke from the trains often made it impossible to see in the tunnels!

Undergrounds around the world
The world's oldest and longest underground is in London, in the UK. It opened in 1863. The underground with the most stations is in New York, in the USA, where there are 452 stops to travel between.

Tickets can be bought from a machine or ticket seller.

Automatic gates open when you put your ticket in the slot.

Moving staircases, called escalators, take you to the platforms.

Staff in the control room watch the trains and the platforms on video screens.

Emergency stairs can be used if the escalators break down.

Large maps on the walls help you to plan your journey.

▼ Beneath busy city streets, underground railways help to keep people moving.

Rush hour
Twice a day, in cities all over the world, thousands of people travel to and from work. This is called the rush hour and is the busiest time on the underground.

▲ In Tokyo, in Japan, the rush hour is so busy that people called 'shovers' try to push more passengers inside the train.

The Channel Tunnel
Not all underground trains run under cities. The Channel Tunnel in Europe, which links England to France, runs under the sea. It was opened in 1994 and is 50km long.

Quiz Corner
● Where is the world's oldest and longest underground?

● What is the name of the tunnel between England and France?

● What are 'shovers', and where do they work?

look at: Animal power, page 4

Travelling over snow

In cold northern countries, such as Lapland and Alaska, the ground is usually covered with ice and snow. This makes it difficult for people to travel by car. Instead, they use **vehicles** that are specially designed to travel over snowy or icy ground.

Travelling across snow and ice
In the past, sleds carried people and goods across icy, northern lands. The sleds were pulled by a team of husky dogs. Today, people usually prefer to travel in snowmobiles, which are powered by an **engine**.

SEE FOR YOURSELF

Snowshoes are wider and flatter than ordinary shoes. This stops them from sinking into the snow. Try this test for yourself. Cut out a large shoe shape from card and tie it to your foot. Keep your other foot bare and then walk across some sand. Which foot sinks?

▼ This sled driver is shouting instructions to his dogs. The number of dogs pulling the sled depends on the load.

▲ A snowmobile moves along on two skis, which help it to glide smoothly over icy ground.

Cross-country skiing

In snowy countries, such as Denmark, Norway and Finland, cross-country skiing is one of the cheapest and quickest ways to travel. It also keeps people fit. At the winter Olympics, there are downhill, cross-country and ski-jumping competitions.

▲ Skiing can be an exciting winter sport.

Quiz Corner

● What kind of transport do people often use today to travel across icy lands?

● Why is skiing a good way of travelling in some countries?

● Why are snowshoes wider than ordinary shoes?

look at: Cars, page 10, Buses and trams, page 12

In the future

Cars, buses, trucks and trains are always being improved to make journeys faster, safer and more comfortable. Fumes from motor **engines** can harm the **environment**, so it is important to use public transport, which saves **fuel** and reduces **pollution**.

Energy of the future
Many people are developing new types of transport which use different kinds of **energy**, including electricity. Solar-powered cars take their energy from the heat and light of the Sun.

▶ Special panels on this car turn energy from the Sun into **power**.

▲ This car, designed in France, saves fuel by travelling vast distances on a drop of petrol.

Keeping things moving

New traffic control systems are being designed to help keep **vehicles** moving on busy roads. Cameras and computers can let traffic police know about problems, such as traffic jams and accidents, so they can quickly go to help.

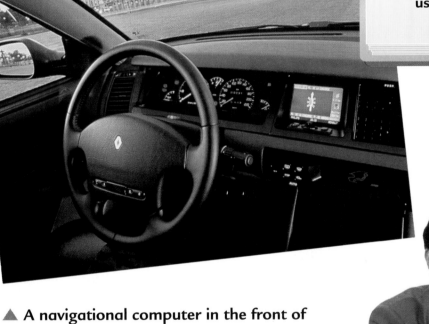

▲ A navigational computer in the front of a car can tell a driver the best **route** to take and warn of traffic jams ahead.

What next?

All the time, scientists are busy designing different vehicles to carry people and goods. These new types of transport might look strange now, but soon you might see them in towns and cities everywhere.

▶ This tiny car fits inside a special suitcase. When it is not being driven, it can be folded away and carried.

Quiz Corner

● How do solar-powered cars make their energy?

● Why is it important to use public transport?

● Why are navigational computers useful for drivers?

Amazing facts

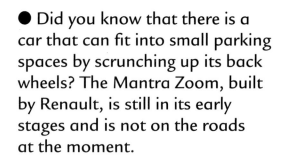

● Did you know that there is a car that can fit into small parking spaces by scrunching up its back wheels? The Mantra Zoom, built by Renault, is still in its early stages and is not on the roads at the moment.

☆ *The power of an engine is measured in units called horsepower. This is because the power of an engine is compared to the pulling power of a horse — so a one horsepower engine is as powerful as one horse.*

● Huskies really need their thick coats to keep them warm. At night, these dogs do not sleep in kennels, but dig themselves a bed in the snow.

☆ *In Italy, there is a train that has been specially designed to lean inwards when it goes round corners. This means that the train does not have to slow down so much for bends, making journeys faster.*

● The largest railway station in the world is Grand Central Station in New York, in the USA. It is built on two levels with 41 tracks on the upper level and 26 on the lower level.

☆ *An American called Henry Ford was the first car manufacturer to build cars on an assembly line. Here, ready-made parts for each car are fitted together at different places along a moving line. Each mechanic has to do just one job, so the cars can be built more quickly.*

● The world's longest car is a 26-wheeled limousine, built in California, in the USA. It is over 30m long and has an enormous water bed and a swimming pool in the back.

☆ *Mexico City has some of the world's worst traffic jams! It also has over 60,000 taxis, which is more than any other city in the world.*

Glossary

deck Each floor of a **vehicle**, such as a bus.

diesel A type of oil used in some **engines**.

energy What gives people and machines the **power** to do a job, for example to make an **engine** go.

engine A machine that changes **energy** into the **power** to do a job.

environment The world around us.

freight Goods moved from place to place by train or truck.

friction When two surfaces rub together, there is friction. When tyres rub against the surface of a road, friction slows down the wheels.

fuel Any substance that is burnt to make heat or **energy**. **Engines** need fuel to make them work.

gear This changes the speed at which the wheels of a **vehicle** go round, so it is easier to go up hills.

pollute To spoil clean air, soil or water with dirty and harmful things.

pollution Dirt and unhealthy things in the **environment**.

power The strength to do a job.

route The way you take to travel to a particular place.

siren A machine which makes a warning sound on an emergency **vehicle**.

spokes Thin bars that join the centre, or hub, of a wheel to its outside, or rim.

streamlined A smooth, rounded shape that lets air or water flow easily over it. A racing car has a streamlined shape to make it faster than a normal car.

tread The bumpy pattern on a tyre, which helps the wheel to get a good grip on the road. The tread on a tyre also pushes water away, making tyres less likely to slip on wet roads.

vehicle A form of transport that moves people or goods from one place to another.

Index

A
ambulance **19**
animal **4-5, 17, 26, 30**
articulated truck **14**

B
Benz, Karl **10**
bicycle **6-7**
building site **16**
bulldozer **16**
bus **12-13**
bypass **21**

C
car **10-11, 18, 20, 21, 26, 28, 29, 30**
car transporter **15**
cement mixer **16**
Channel Tunnel **25**
coach **13**
combine harvester **17**
crane **16**

D
Daimler, Gottlieb **8**
digger **17**

E
elephant **5**
emergency vehicle **18-19**
energy **10, 28**

F
farm vehicle **17**
fire engine **18-19**
flyover **20**
Ford, Henry **30**
freight train **23**
freight truck **14-15**
friction **9**
fuel **10, 12, 14, 28**

H
horse **4**
horsepower **30**
husky dogs **26, 30**

I
ice **26**

L
llama **4, 5**

M
monorail train **22**
motorbike **8-9**
motorway **20**

P
petrol engine **8, 10**
police car **18**
pollution **6, 13, 24, 28**
public transport **12, 28**

R
racing car **11**
railway station **30**
refrigerator truck **14**
rickshaw **7**
road **20-21**
road train **15**
rush hour **25**

S
skiing **27**
sled **26**
snow **26-27**
snowmobile **26**
snowshoe **26**
solar power **28**
stagecoach **4**
Stephenson's 'Rocket' **23**
streamlined vehicle **10, 14**

T
tanker **15**
tipper truck **16, 17**
traffic jam **11, 24, 29, 30**
trail bike **9**
train **22-23, 30**
tram **13**
truck **14-15, 16-17, 18, 19**
tyre **7, 9, 16**

U
underground train **24-25**

W
wheel **4, 22**

Created by:
Two-Can Publishing Ltd
346 Old Street
London EC1V 9NQ
and Eljay Yildirim of Thunderbolt, London

Text: Deborah Chancellor
Consultant: Eryl Davies
Watercolour artwork: Colin King and Stuart Trotter
Computer artwork: D Oliver

This edition published 1997 by:
Two-Can Publishing
in association with
Franklin Watts
96 Leonard Street
London EC2A 4RH

Hardback ISBN 1-85434-410-2
Dewey Decimal Classification 388

2 4 6 8 10 9 7 5 3 1

A catalogue record for this book is available from the British Library.

Printed in the USA by
R. R. Donnelley & Sons Co.

Photographic credits: Britstock-IFA p15tr, p27tl; Colorific p26bl; Hutchison Library (H.R. Dorig) p4tr; Image Bank p14bl, p17tl, p19tr; A.C. Press p29br; Quadrant p14bc; Spectrum p5; Tony Stone Images p8b, p22-23c, p25tr; Frank Spooner p28b&t, p29tl; Telegraph Colour Library p18bl; Zefa Pictures FC, p6bl, p7cr, p9, p11t, p12, p26-27bc.